GW00858457

# OWL'S NEW CARDS

## by Kathryn Ernst

## pictures by Diane deGroat

Crown Publishers, Inc., New York

The text of this book is set in 14 point Koronna. The illustrations are charcoal drawings, printed in three
colors, with pencil shaded overlays prepared by the artist.

Library of Congress Cataloging in Publication Data
Ernst, Kathryn F.
    Owl's new cards.
    Summary: Owl makes a new deck of cards for the daily
games with Brown Bear and Rat.
    [1. Cards—Fiction.  2. Animals—Fiction.
3. Friendship—Fiction]  I. De Groat, Diane.  II. Title.
PZ7.E7320w    [E]    77-2652
ISBN 0-517-53090-2

To my darling and
very clever card player,
Alexandra Ernst

Owl, Brown Bear, and Rat were best friends. They made up songs together. They took camping trips together. And every night at five o'clock they played cards together. But one night Owl's wings drooped. "Oh, no!" he said. "The Queen of Clubs is missing."

"So is the Two of Spades," said Rat quietly.

"This card's been chewed," said Brown Bear, holding up the Six of Diamonds.

"That's what I get for lending them to Squirrel," said Owl. "I'll never do that again."

Rat patted Owl on the head. "Don't worry. We'll find another deck. Campers are always leaving them behind."

"But camping season is almost over," said Owl.

"He's right," said Brown Bear.

The three friends sat silently wondering what to do. Finally Rat said, "We'll think of something."

Owl brightened. "Sure," he said. "We'll think of something."

Brown Bear pointed to the autumn leaves overhead. "We'd better do it fast," she said.

Owl and Rat knew Brown Bear was right. Once winter came, there would be no campers, no hunters, no hikers, and no bird watchers.

Owl sighed as Brown Bear picked up Rat and put him on her shoulder. "Good night," he said.

Late that night Owl's sharp eyes searched the forest for a new deck of cards. Twice he thought he saw something. But it turned out to be an empty cigarette pack and an old torn map. Then he had an idea. "I'll make the cards myself," he said. "They'll be beautiful!" He was so excited he nearly flew into a branch on his way home.

The next day Owl worked very hard. He gathered pieces of birchbark and carefully cut them into cards. Then he painted each one. By five o'clock he had not slept a wink but he had a beautiful new deck of cards. There wasn't another deck like it in the world.

The Jacks all looked like Rat.
The Queens looked like Brown Bear.
The Kings looked like Owl himself.

Owl was proud and pleased. "Oh,
happy us," he sang. He pictured Brown
Bear giving him a big hug and Rat
smiling shyly.

But five o'clock passed and Rat and Brown Bear did not come.

Owl looked at his clock. "That's odd," he said. "They're usually on time." He flew down to the ground and sat on a rock. "Oh, well," he said, "there is no reason to get upset. They'll be here soon."

By 5:30 Owl could not sit still any longer. He walked around in circles. Then he thought, "I'll make some sweet tea. Brown Bear and Rat love sweet tea."

At 5:45 Owl set a big pot of steaming tea on the table and laid out three cups and saucers. But Brown Bear and Rat still did not come.

"I wonder what has happened," thought Owl. He flew to the top of his tree and looked around. There was no one in sight. "This can't be," he said. "Where are they?" He thought about going to look for them. But he was afraid he would miss them if he left his tree.

By 6:00 Owl was hurt and angry. "I can't believe this," he said. "They have stood me up!" Part of him felt like crying. Part of him felt like screeching. So he stood beneath his tree stomping his foot. "They don't care about me!" he said. "They just care about playing cards." He grabbed the deck in his claws. "I'll show them," he shouted. "They're not my only friends."

Owl flew deep into the woods and circled high above Big Pond. He spotted Beaver, whistling and whizzing down a mud slide. Owl usually did not like to play with Beaver. But this night Owl didn't care.

"How about a game of War?" he asked as he landed near Beaver's slide.

Beaver climbed out of the water. "Sure," he said. "It's my favorite game."

Owl fluffed his feathers and dealt the cards into two equal piles. "I made these cards myself," he said.

"Not bad," said Beaver. But he did not even look at them.

"Don't you like them?" asked Owl.

Beaver did not answer. He turned over his first card. It was the Queen of Hearts. "Ho! Ho!" he yelled. "This is my lucky day!"

"You don't have to shout," said Owl. Then he turned over his first card. It was the Four of Clubs.

"I won!" shouted Beaver. "I knew I would!" He grabbed Owl's card and put it into his pile.

"Hey!" said Owl. "Don't bend the cards." But the next three rounds weren't any better. Owl did not win once and Beaver kept bending the cards.

"I'm so good at this," said Beaver happily. He slapped his tail and bits of mud flew all over the place.

"Stop it," said Owl. "You're getting mud on the cards."

"I am not," said Beaver.

"You are too," said Owl. "You're mean!"

Beaver did not say a word. He simply stuck out his two front teeth, threw down the cards, and dove into the water.

"Come back," shouted Owl. "The game isn't over yet!" But Beaver was already swimming toward his home at the bottom of Big Pond.

Owl sat on the grass and blinked. He felt awful. He slowly picked up his cards and started for home.

On the way he saw Weasel. Weasel was sitting by his burrow playing jacks and singing softly to himself.

"How about a game of cards?" asked Owl.

"Great," said Weasel. "I just learned a new game."

"What's it called?" asked Owl.

"Fifty-two pickup," said Weasel. He rubbed his paws

together and grinned. "I'll teach you."

"Okay," said Owl, "but please be careful with the cards. I just made them."

"Of course," said Weasel. Weasel shuffled the cards and put them into a neat pile. "Now watch," he said.

Weasel picked up the pile, raised his paws, and threw the cards into the air.

Owl couldn't believe his eyes. "MY CARDS!" he shouted. "WHAT DID YOU DO THAT FOR?"

Weasel was holding his sides and shaking with laughter. "It's a joke," he said. "There are fifty-two cards in the deck and you have to pick them all up. Get it? Fifty-two pickup."

Owl flew toward Weasel but Weasel darted into his burrow. "A JOKE!" screeched Owl. "THAT'S NOT A JOKE!" His feathers were flying and he was screeching so loudly that Brown Bear and Rat heard him all the way on the other side of the forest.

Rat grabbed onto Brown Bear's fur. They ran in the direction of the noise. When they found Owl, he was standing in front of Weasel's hole, crying and yelling.

Rat tugged on Owl's wing. "What's wrong?" he asked.

"Weasel threw my new cards all over the place," yelled Owl.

"New cards?" said Rat. He bent down and picked some of them up. "Why…these are beautiful," he said. "And…why…this one looks just like me!"

"That's because I made it that way," sniffed Owl.

"This one looks like me!" said Brown Bear. "Owl! These are fantastic!"

Owl stopped crying. "Do you really like them?"

"Oh, yes," said Rat.

"Then why didn't you come tonight?" Owl demanded. "I was waiting to show you the cards! I even made sweet tea!"

"We were out looking for cards," said Brown Bear. "We wanted to surprise you."

"We walked all the way to Long Mountain," said Rat.

"Really?" said Owl.

"We tried to find you when we got back," said Rat. "But you weren't home."

"Gee," said Owl. He suddenly felt ashamed and embarrassed.

"You're our best friend," said Brown Bear.

"I am?" said Owl.

"Of course," said Rat. "You know that."

The three friends picked up all the cards and went to Brown Bear's house. They took turns dealing the cards and played all their favorite games. Everyone had a good time, especially Owl, who thought that Brown Bear and Rat were the nicest friends an Owl could have.

# what we

# Plumber

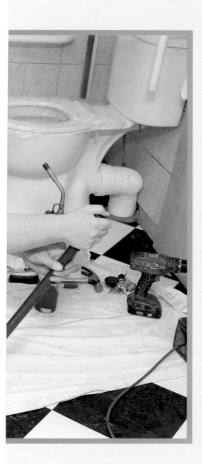

PHOTOGRAPHY BY BOBBY HUMPHREY

## W
### FRANKLIN WATTS
LONDON•SYDNEY

This edition published in 2014 by

Franklin Watts
338 Euston Road
London NW1 3BH

Franklin Watts Australia
Level 17/207 Kent Street
Sydney, NSW 2000

Planning and production by
Discovery Books Limited
Editor: James Nixon
Design: sprout.uk.com
Commissioned photography: Bobby Humphrey

Dewey number: 696.1'023

ISBN: 978 1 4451 2948 8

Printed in China

Franklin Watts is a division of Hachette
Children's Books, an Hachette UK company.

www.hachette.co.uk

Acknowledgements: Shutterstock Images:
pp. 16 middle (Marek R Swadzba), 16 bottom
left (noolwlee), 16 bottom right (Garsya),
23 (nostal6ie).

The author, packager and publisher would like
to thank Damselfly Female Heating and
Plumbing Services, Leeds, for their help and
participation in this book.

# what we do

# CONTENTS

Words in **bold** appear in the glossary on page 24.

# I AM A PLUMBER

My name is Karen. I work as a plumber. I fix, install and maintain the pipe systems, called plumbing, in people's homes. The pipes provide water and heating, so the job I do is very important.

A box of tools is a plumber's most important possession. It contains a wide range of equipment including **wrenches**, spanners, pliers, blow torches, **gauges**, and pipe cutters and benders. The tools I use depend on the type of job I'm doing. I could be fixing a leaking pipe, unblocking a sink or fitting a new washing machine.

▼ *When I install a washbasin I have to attach supply and waste pipes to the basin to carry the water.*

*◄ Plumbers have to be fairly fit, and happy to work in all kinds of conditions, including dirty and cramped spaces.*

Like many plumbers I am self-employed. This means I am my own boss and I have to arrange work and organise the **business** myself.

I am on the move a lot of the time, dashing from one job to the next. I am always busy and sometimes I work at the weekends. My phone rings many times a day with people asking me to do a job or come out to deal with an emergency.

I enjoy the job because of the variety of work and different people I meet. The downside of my job is keeping up with the paperwork and chasing payments from my customers.

## KEY SKILLS

**DEXTERITY** – This means being skilled at working with your hands. This is important for a plumber using tools and materials.

# FINDING WORK

Some plumbers work for a firm. If you are self-employed like me you have to find jobs for yourself. The best way to get more work is to do an excellent job and then the customer will recommend you to their friends and family.

Plumbers have to be good with people as well as their hands. If I am friendly, chatty and honest it is more likely that my name will get passed around.

It is very important to be polite and **respect** people's homes. I am careful not to cause any damage and to leave the place as clean and tidy as when I arrived. I also make sure that I am reliable and turn up for jobs on time.

◄ *I show customers my card so that they recognise who I am.*

I listen carefully to the customers so that I understand exactly the work they would like me to do. Then I can be sure that they will be happy with the end result. This woman wants me to **renovate** her bathroom. I answer her questions, give my professional advice and suggest ways in which I could create the bathroom she wants.

▲ *I advise the customer which type of shower I think would be best to install.*

## KEY SKILLS

**GOOD COMMUNICATION –**
**You must communicate clearly**
**with the customers so that they**
**understand your advice.**

# PLANNING A PROJECT

Buildings are always being altered, repaired or **erected** so there is a high demand for plumbers like me. When I start a project, sometimes I have to study drawings and **blueprints** or plan the layout of pipes and appliances myself.

This man wants a toilet for disabled people installed in an office block. He shows me the plans and I read them so that I can negotiate the cost for doing the job.

▼ *The blueprints tell me exactly where the customer wants the plumbing to be fixed.*

Plumbers need to have good maths skills. When I am planning a project I take lots of measurements and have to do calculations in my head.

*▲ I have to be extremely accurate with my measurements. One wrong measurement can mess up the whole plan!*

Back at my house I have an office where I prepare a **quote**. This tells the customer how much I think it will cost to have the work done. The price I give depends on the materials I will have to use, and how long I estimate the job will take.

*▶ The quote I prepare has to make me some profit, but also be a price that is fair for the customer.*

# PIPE FITTING

Fitting new pipes is a large part of my job. Copper and plastic are the two most common materials used for pipes in household plumbing. I use a variety of tools and methods to cut, bend and join pipes.

## TOOLS OF THE TRADE

When I cut the pipes to the right length I make sure the ends are cut square and smooth. This is a pipe cutter (right). I put the tool around the copper pipe and twist it in my hand to cut.

You can also bend pipes around corners. I insert the pipe into a bending machine and squeeze the handles together until the pipe is curved to the angle I want.

◄ *Copper is quite a soft metal and can be bent into shape with a little force.*

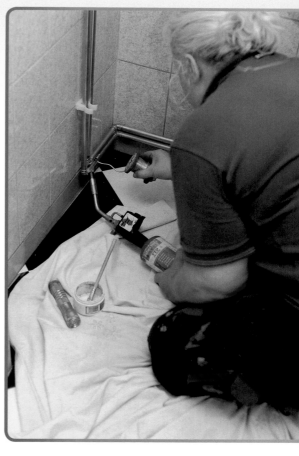

There are different kinds of connecting parts to join the pipes. Some can be fastened with spanners. Here, I am sealing a joint with a blow torch (above). This heats the metal, and then I melt soft **solder** wire on to it until the joint is fused together (above right).

▲ *I melt the wire until there is a ring of solder all round the joint.*

When you join pipes it is important to clean the ends of the pipes so that they join firmly. I am coating this plastic pipe with a sticky **cement** to join it to another (left).

## KEY SKILLS

**ATTENTION TO DETAIL –
To work neatly and accurately
you need a good eye for detail.**

# FIXING LEAKS

Leaking pipes and equipment are jobs that need urgent attention. Pipes sometimes burst in very cold weather because the water in them expands as it turns to ice.

## KEY SKILLS

**ABILITY TO SOLVE PROBLEMS**
– Logical thinking will help you find faults and fix them.

This pipe (left top) has a small split in it. I have to remove the damaged section and replace it. To fasten the new piece of pipe I tighten the nuts at each end (left middle). The seal at the back of the **stopcock** is also leaking. I wind some plastic tape over the leak and push it into place with the tip of a screwdriver blade to create a new seal (below).

▲▼ *I use one spanner to hold the pipe securely and another to tighten the nut. The new pipe (below) will not leak.*

12

Locating damaged pipes is sometimes a hard job. Pipes can be found in the loft, behind tiles or under floorboards (below).

I also test pipes for leaks if I suspect there might be a problem somewhere in the system. I have a gauge that tells me the **pressure** of the water in the pipes. If the pressure is too low then I know there is a problem.

▲ *This gauge tells me the pressure of the gas in the pipes and can identify a leak.*

I am qualified to work with gas. Leaking gas is very dangerous, so I have another gauge which can detect if gas is in the air.

◄ *The detector can pinpoint even the tiniest amount of gas leaking from an appliance.*

13

# CLEARING BLOCKAGES

I sometimes get called out to clean out blockages in waste pipes. Hairs, grease and other bits that go down the plughole can clog up the pipes.

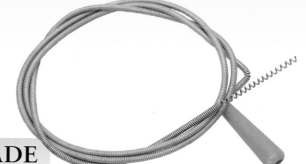

## TOOLS OF THE TRADE

If the water in a sink will not run away I use a sink auger (above right) to probe the pipe and dislodge anything that is blocking it. If this doesn't work, the blockage must be further down the pipe. I then have to take the pipe apart underneath the sink and poke the auger from there.

When I take pipes apart I use a bucket to catch any water in the system. Plumbing can be a dirty, messy job at times. It is not uncommon to be sprayed from water in a pipe. Sometimes I have to clear blockages and leaks in a toilet pan.

▶ *Plumbers are careful not to get themselves or their work area wet.*

## KEY SKILLS

**FITNESS AND AGILITY –**
You will need strength to lift heavy objects and **agility** to work in tight spaces.

◀ *Lifting a radiator into and out of place is hard work.*

I enjoy the challenge of working in tricky environments. Crouching under sinks and working in dark, dusty places, such as under floorboards, can be uncomfortable. I work outdoors, too, sometimes in cold and wet conditions. When I am fixing guttering I need a head for heights (below).

# KITCHENS AND BATHROOMS

I spend a lot of my time installing appliances and fittings that use water or gas, such as sinks, baths, showers, dishwashers, cookers (right) and central heating systems.

To install a new dishwasher or washing machine I have to connect pipes from the back of the appliance to the hot and cold water supply, and another pipe from the machine to the waste pipe so the dirty water can drain away.

## TOOLS OF THE TRADE

To connect the pipes to the water supply I first have to remove a segment from each supply pipe. I cut the pipes out squarely with a small hacksaw (above). The new pipes are then joined to the water supply via T-junction connectors, like this one (left). I tighten the nuts on the joints with a spanner (below). This spanner can be adjusted so that it fits the nut exactly.

▲ *A new toilet has to be put in level so that it flushes properly.*

Here (above), I am installing a toilet for disabled people in a new building. I have to put all the supply and drainage pipes in, as well as fix the toilet and washbasin to the wall.

On major projects I sometimes work with other **tradespeople**, such as plasterers and electricians. This electrician is helping me to install the electric shower and the lighting (right).

## KEY SKILLS

METHODICAL –To do a good job you need to approach your work carefully and **methodically.**

# GAINING EXPERIENCE

If you think plumbing might be the right job for you it is a good idea to do some kind of work experience. Then if you decide you like the job you can start to earn your qualifications.

▲ *There is no better way to learn than by watching the experts.*

Ask the plumbers in your local area if you can **shadow** them for a few days. This will give you an idea of the day-to-day life of a plumber. You could also offer to help a friend or relative who is doing some **DIY** plumbing in their house. I found out I enjoyed plumbing while I was fitting my own bathroom. The more I learned, the more confident I was that this was the job for me.

## KEY SKILLS

**ABILITY TO WORK ON YOUR OWN** – Once you are a fully trained plumber you work largely by yourself.

You need a lot of skill and knowledge to be a plumber. Any experience you gain will give you a head start when you come to do your training. One route into a plumbing career is through an apprenticeship with a small or large firm. Here, you take your qualifications at college at the same time as having a paid, hands-on job.

Apprenticeships are highly sought after, and there is a lot of competition for places. You will have a big advantage if you can show employers that you have plumbing experience and practical skills. Some employers require school leavers to have gained four GCSEs or above.

▼ *Apprentices start off by learning basic tasks, such as fixing a leaking tap. Even when you are learning, your work must be of a high standard.*

# QUALIFICATIONS

You can learn how to become a plumber at a local college or training centre without an apprenticeship. That is what I did. Once you have completed your qualifications you can start earning money as a tradesperson.

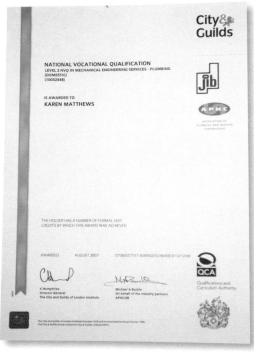

The qualifications you need are the *NVQ Diploma in Plumbing and Domestic Heating* at *Level 2* (above) and *Level 3*. These are provided by City and Guilds or EAL. The course starts with knowledge-based lessons and then progresses to practical units which are done on a **work placement**. *Level 2* covers basic plumbing while *Level 3* teaches you how to work with fuels such as gas.

◀ *Making pipework to carry rainwater from the roof of a house is one of many jobs you learn during a* Level 2 NVQ.

There are lots of water and building regulations that you must learn. Regulations are rules that we have to stick to when we carry out our work. For example, when I install a tap a one-way valve must be fitted. This stops dirty water going up into the tap and keeps the water clean and safe to drink.

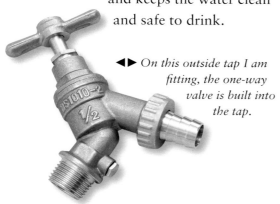

*◄► On this outside tap I am fitting, the one-way valve is built into the tap.*

By providing fresh water and proper drainage we play an important role in the public's health. As we carry out work, we have to look after our own safety, too. I wear safety goggles when I operate power tools (left).

## KEY SKILLS

**WILLINGNESS TO LEARN – You have to constantly learn as a plumber as the products and technologies are always changing.**

# GETTING ON

Plumbers who only work with water are called wet-only plumbers. To work with gas legally you have to pass an assessment which puts you on the Gas Safe Register. I have an ID card, like the one below, which shows customers that I am on the register and can safely work on their gas appliances.

▲ *I make sure all the radiators heat up properly when I service a home's central heating.*

I **service** gas boilers that provide people with central heating for their homes. Some plumbers are trained to service and repair oil-fired heating systems and cookers.

◄ *All boilers should be serviced regularly by experts only.*

■ With further training you can learn how to install and maintain **renewable** energy technologies, such as solar powered heating systems. Not all plumbers work in a domestic setting. Some work for large companies and work on pipe systems in big gas plants or other industries, such as shipbuilding and chemical production.

▲ *There are many routes a plumber can take. You can work in industrial places rather than people's homes.*

■ There are all kinds of areas that plumbers can move into. You can specialise in air conditioning or **refrigeration** systems. Experience counts for a lot in plumbing as there is so much to learn. The Chartered Institute of Plumbing and Heating Engineering (CIPHE) awards a certificate to plumbers who have worked to a high standard for over ten years. If you receive this you become a Master Plumber!

## KEY SKILLS

**DETERMINATION – You need to have ambition and drive to advance your career.**

# GLOSSARY

**agility** The skill of being able to move your body easily.

**blueprint** A drawing showing a design plan.

**business** Work relating to selling a service and making a profit.

**cement** A soft glue which hardens when it sets.

**DIY** Decorating or repairing your own home. DIY stands for 'Do It Yourself'.

**erect** To build something.

**gauge** An instrument which measures the level of something.

**methodically** Methodical means to work orderly and carefully to a fixed plan.

**pressure** The force that is produced when something is pushed, such as gas or water in a pipe.

**quote** The estimated price for a job.

**refrigeration** A process which keeps something cool by taking the heat away from it.

**renewable** Describes an energy source that will not run out, such as the wind or the Sun.

**renovate** Restore or repair something to a good condition.

**respect** Avoid harming and interfering with.

**service** A routine inspection and maintenance of a machine.

**shadow** Follow someone and watch them closely.

**solder** A wire mainly made from tin, which can be melted to fuse other metals together.

**stopcock** A tap that can turn a house's water supply on or off.

**tradespeople** People who do jobs that require skills with their hands.

**work placement** A temporary post to gain work experience.

**wrench** A tool used for gripping and turning nuts or bolts.

# INDEX